CHILDREN'S STORYTELLERS

Lois Lowry

by Chris Bowman

BELLWETHER MEDIA • MINNEAPOLIS, MN

Note to Librarians, Teachers, and Parents:

Blastoff! Readers are carefully developed by literacy experts and combine standards-based content with developmentally appropriate text.

Level 1 provides the most support through repetition of high-frequency words, light text, predictable sentence patterns, and strong visual support.

Level 2 offers early readers a bit more challenge through varied simple sentences, increased text load, and less repetition of high-frequency words.

Level 3 advances early-fluent readers toward fluency through increased text and concept load, less reliance on visuals, longer sentences, and more literary language.

Level 4 builds reading stamina by providing more text per page, increased use of punctuation, greater variation in sentence patterns, and increasingly challenging vocabulary.

Level 5 encourages children to move from "learning to read" to "reading to learn" by providing even more text, varied writing styles, and less familiar topics.

Whichever book is right for your reader, Blastoff! Readers are the perfect books to build confidence and encourage a love of reading that will last a lifetime!

This edition first published in 2016 by Bellwether Media, Inc.

No part of this publication may be reproduced in whole or in part without written permission of the publisher. For information regarding permission, write to Bellwether Media, Inc., Attention: Permissions Department, 5357 Penn Avenue South, Minneapolis, MN 55419.

Library of Congress Cataloging-in-Publication Data

Bowman, Chris, 1990-
  Lois Lowry / by Chris Bowman.
    pages cm – (Blastoff! Readers: Children's Storytellers)
  Summary: "Simple text and full-color photographs introduce readers to Lois Lowry. Developed by literacy experts for students in second through fifth grade"– Provided by publisher.
  Includes bibliographical references and index.
  ISBN 978-1-62617-340-8 (hardcover : alk. paper)
  1. Lowry, Lois–Juvenile literature. 2. Authors, American–20th century–Biography–Juvenile literature. 3. Children's literature–Authorship–Juvenile literature. I. Title.
  PS3562.O923Z63 2016
  813'.54–dc23
  [B]   2015000855

Printed in the United States of America, North Mankato, MN.

Table of Contents

Lois Lowry is an award-winning author of children's and young adult books. She has written more than 40 books in her **career** of about 40 years.

Two of her **novels**, *The Giver* and *Number the Stars*, have won **Newbery Medals**. Lois's many books delight young readers all over the world!

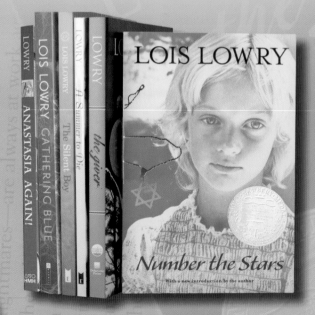

On the Move

Lois was born on March 20, 1937, in Honolulu, Hawaii. Lois's father was in the military. The family moved around often.

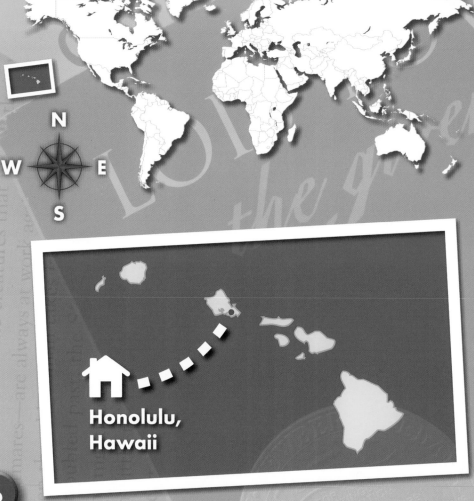

Honolulu,
Hawaii

Lois became interested in books at a young age. Her older sister, Helen, helped her learn to read and write by the time she was 3 years old. Instead of playing with other kids, Lois read and daydreamed.

When she started school, Lois was already an advanced reader. She attended kindergarten in Brooklyn, New York, but her family soon moved to Pennsylvania. There, she skipped a grade so she would be challenged more.

Even so, Lois preferred going to the public library over school. By the time she was 8 years old, she knew she wanted to be a writer.

A TREE GROWS IN BROOKLYN

BETTY SMITH

HARPERPERENNIAL ◆ MODERNCLASSICS

fun fact

Lois was limited to one library visit per day. Because of this, she checked out thick books. One of her favorites was *A Tree Grows in Brooklyn* by Betty Smith.

"I read everything. I was lucky that I grew up in a family that valued books. I went to the library all the time starting at about age 5 or 6. My mom read to me. I read to myself."

Lois Lowry

Lois's Chosen Career

In 1948, Lois's family moved to Tokyo, Japan. The experience opened Lois's eyes to new **cultures**. The family returned to the United States after two years. There, Lois began high school.

"Reading is the best way to learn to write well."
Lois Lowry

Brown
University

fun fact

Lois's high school classmates guessed she would go on to be a writer.

She began studying **creative writing** at Brown University in 1954. After her second year, she left school to get married. She followed her husband, Donald, who had just joined the U.S. Navy.

11

Lois and Donald's family grew quickly. The couple had four kids in six years. Lois stayed home with her children. But she never gave up on her dreams.

! fun fact

Lois and Donald moved around for his job. They lived in California, Connecticut, Florida, South Carolina, Massachusetts, and Maine.

In 1968, Lois went back to college. She studied **literature** and photography. After graduating, she wrote **nonfiction** for magazines, newspapers, and textbooks. Her first short story was **published** in 1975.

Lois's short story caught the eye of a children's book editor. She asked Lois to try writing for kids. In 1977, *A Summer to Die* was published.

Soon after, Lois and Donald divorced. But Lois continued writing. Her second book came out the next year. For many years, she wrote one or two books each year. Her dream of being a successful author had come true!

fun fact

Lois's photography appears on the covers of some of her books. These include *The Giver* and *Number the Stars*.

Giving Important Lessons

Lois writes stories in many styles. Some of her books are serious. Others are funny. All of them focus on human relationships. She wants readers to see how people need one another.

SELECTED WORKS

A Summer to Die (1977)

Anastasia Krupnik (1979)

Number the Stars (1989)

The Giver (1993)

Gathering Blue (2000)

The Silent Boy (2003)

Messenger (2004)

Gossamer (2006)

The Willoughbys (2008)

Son (2012)

> "Everything a writer experiences as a young person goes into the later writing in some form."
>
> Lois Lowry

Family and friendship are common **themes** for Lois. Some of her books explore the feelings of losing loved ones. She wrote *A Summer to Die* about losing her sister at a young age.

Many of Lois's stories are also funny.
The Anastasia Krupnik **series**
sometimes covers heavy topics.
But it is usually light-hearted.

Lois balances the serious subjects with humor and silly situations. She reminds readers that laughter is important.

POP CULTURE CONNECTION

In 2014, *The Giver* movie came out in theaters. Stars such as Meryl Streep and Jeff Bridges helped bring the book to the big screen.

"I deal with the frustrations, fears, and disappointments of life by making stories out of them."
Lois Lowry

Coloring Our World

Lois's books are favorites for many children and teens. They challenge readers to think about life's questions, big and small.

"Anything that makes you think: 'What if?' is the start of a story."
Lois Lowry

IMPORTANT DATES

1937: Lois Lowry is born in Hawaii on March 20.

1972: Lois graduates from the University of Southern Maine.

1977: Lois's first children's book, *A Summer to Die*, is published.

1978: Lois receives the Children's Book Award from the International Reading Association.

1983: Lois is a National Book Award Finalist for *Anastasia Again!*

1987: The Boston Globe-Horn Book Award is awarded to *Rabble Starkey*.

1990: *Number the Stars* receives the Newbery Medal.

1994: The Newbery Medal is awarded to *The Giver*.

2007: Lois receives the Margaret A. Edwards Award for her contributions to young adult literature.

Lois is currently working on her next book. She continues to give kids new ways to see the world around them!

Glossary

career—a job someone does for a long time

creative writing—the study of how to write stories and poems

cultures—the specific beliefs and practices of a group or region

literature—written works, often books, that are highly respected

Newbery Medals—awards given each year to the best American children's books; the Newbery Medal is given to first place and the runners-up receive Newbery Honors.

nonfiction—writing that is about facts or real events

novels—longer written stories, usually about made-up characters and events

published—printed for a public audience

series—a number of things that are connected in a certain order

themes—important ideas or messages

To Learn More

AT THE LIBRARY

Erlic, Lily. *Lois Lowry.* New York, N.Y.: AV2 by Weigl, 2013.

Lowry, Lois. *Looking Back: A Book of Memories.* Boston, Mass.: Houghton Mifflin, 1998.

Lowry, Lois. *Number the Stars.* Boston, Mass.: Houghton Mifflin Harcourt, 2014.

ON THE WEB

Learning more about Lois Lowry is as easy as 1, 2, 3.

1. Go to www.factsurfer.com.

2. Enter "Lois Lowry" into the search box.

3. Click the "Surf" button and you will see a list of related web sites.

With factsurfer.com, finding more information is just a click away.

Index

The images in this book are reproduced through the courtesy of: Robin Platzer/ Twin Images/ Newscom, front cover (left); Yeng Moua, front cover (right); Domini Brown, pp. 4, 8, 14, 15, 16, 21; Boston Globe/ Getty Images, pp. 5, 18, 20; Ricardo DeAratanha/ Getty Images, p. 7 (top); Twin Design, p. 7 (bottom); Portland Press Herald/ Getty Images, p. 9; Taylor Hill/ Getty Images, p. 10; Tupungato, p. 11; Evan Agostini/ Invision/ AP Images, p. 13; Chance Yeh/ Getty Images, p. 17; The Weinstein Company/ Alamy, p. 19.